TUNISIA'S STRUGGLE FOR STABILITY, SECURITY, AND DEMOCRACY

HEARING

BEFORE THE

SUBCOMMITTEE ON
THE MIDDLE EAST AND NORTH AFRICA

OF THE

COMMITTEE ON FOREIGN AFFAIRS
HOUSE OF REPRESENTATIVES

ONE HUNDRED FOURTEENTH CONGRESS

SECOND SESSION

MAY 25, 2016

Serial No. 114–193

Printed for the use of the Committee on Foreign Affairs

Available via the World Wide Web: http://www.foreignaffairs.house.gov/ or
http://www.gpo.gov/fdsys/

U.S. GOVERNMENT PUBLISHING OFFICE

20–258PDF   WASHINGTON : 2016

For sale by the Superintendent of Documents, U.S. Government Publishing Office
Internet: bookstore.gpo.gov   Phone: toll free (866) 512–1800; DC area (202) 512–1800
Fax: (202) 512–2104   Mail: Stop IDCC, Washington, DC 20402–0001

COMMITTEE ON FOREIGN AFFAIRS

EDWARD R. ROYCE, California, *Chairman*

CHRISTOPHER H. SMITH, New Jersey
ILEANA ROS-LEHTINEN, Florida
DANA ROHRABACHER, California
STEVE CHABOT, Ohio
JOE WILSON, South Carolina
MICHAEL T. McCAUL, Texas
TED POE, Texas
MATT SALMON, Arizona
DARRELL E. ISSA, California
TOM MARINO, Pennsylvania
JEFF DUNCAN, South Carolina
MO BROOKS, Alabama
PAUL COOK, California
RANDY K. WEBER SR., Texas
SCOTT PERRY, Pennsylvania
RON DeSANTIS, Florida
MARK MEADOWS, North Carolina
TED S. YOHO, Florida
CURT CLAWSON, Florida
SCOTT DesJARLAIS, Tennessee
REID J. RIBBLE, Wisconsin
DAVID A. TROTT, Michigan
LEE M. ZELDIN, New York
DANIEL DONOVAN, New York

ELIOT L. ENGEL, New York
BRAD SHERMAN, California
GREGORY W. MEEKS, New York
ALBIO SIRES, New Jersey
GERALD E. CONNOLLY, Virginia
THEODORE E. DEUTCH, Florida
BRIAN HIGGINS, New York
KAREN BASS, California
WILLIAM KEATING, Massachusetts
DAVID CICILLINE, Rhode Island
ALAN GRAYSON, Florida
AMI BERA, California
ALAN S. LOWENTHAL, California
GRACE MENG, New York
LOIS FRANKEL, Florida
TULSI GABBARD, Hawaii
JOAQUIN CASTRO, Texas
ROBIN L. KELLY, Illinois
BRENDAN F. BOYLE, Pennsylvania

AMY PORTER, *Chief of Staff*   THOMAS SHEEHY, *Staff Director*
JASON STEINBAUM, *Democratic Staff Director*

———

SUBCOMMITTEE ON THE MIDDLE EAST AND NORTH AFRICA

ILEANA ROS-LEHTINEN, Florida, *Chairman*

STEVE CHABOT, Ohio
JOE WILSON, South Carolina
DARRELL E. ISSA, California
RANDY K. WEBER SR., Texas
RON DeSANTIS, Florida
MARK MEADOWS, North Carolina
TED S. YOHO, Florida
CURT CLAWSON, Florida
DAVID A. TROTT, Michigan
LEE M. ZELDIN, New York

THEODORE E. DEUTCH, Florida
GERALD E. CONNOLLY, Virginia
BRIAN HIGGINS, New York
DAVID CICILLINE, Rhode Island
ALAN GRAYSON, Florida
GRACE MENG, New York
LOIS FRANKEL, Florida
BRENDAN F. BOYLE, Pennsylvania

CONTENTS

TUNISIA'S STRUGGLE FOR STABILITY, SECURITY, AND DEMOCRACY

WEDNESDAY, MAY 25, 2016

House of Representatives,
Subcommittee on the Middle East and North Africa,
Committee on Foreign Affairs,
Washington, DC.

The subcommittee met, pursuant to notice, at 2:37 p.m., in room 2172, Rayburn House Office Building, Hon. Ileana Ros-Lehtinen (chairman of the subcommittee) presiding.

Ms. Ros-Lehtinen. The subcommittee will come to order.

After recognizing myself and Ranking Member Deutch for 5 minutes, each, for our opening statements, I will then recognize other members seeking recognition for 1 minute.

We will then hear from our witnesses. And without objection, the witnesses' prepared statements will be made a part of the record, and members may have 5 days to insert statements and questions for the record subject to the length limitations in the rules.

The chair now recognizes herself for 5 minutes.

Since 2011, Tunisians have made tremendous strides in overcoming decades of crippling authoritarian rule. Multiple free and fair elections, a modern constitution that enshrines women's rights, a rapidly opening space for freedom of the press, and a rare commitment by Tunisia's major political parties to negotiate and find mutually acceptable middle ground so that the democratic transition can continue. These are all remarkable achievements worthy of praise and admiration by Tunisians and outsiders alike.

But for many Tunisians, the transition is not happening nearly as fast as we would have imagined 5 years ago, as they are increasingly disappointed by what is seen as slow progress. Unemployment rates are high, especially for Tunisian youth and for women, and public administration and democracy are still mired by corruption, delays, and competing interests that too often prevent projects from being implemented.

The current government has made a lot of economic progress for which it deserves a great deal of credit, including passing major banking and investment laws which will go a long way in eventually spurring foreign direct investment and job creation.

However, getting that message out and informing the population about the government's achievements is an enormous challenge on its own. Tunisia's minimally staffed legislature does not have the necessary resources to connect with constituents to explain their efforts, especially to those in the interior.

(1)

And the central government's outreach problems are indicative of the challenges ahead for Tunisia's announced municipal elections in March next year.

Among many issues that need to be solved, the cabinet and the legislature still need to figure out how Tunisia will be divided into municipalities, and there is resistance at all levels to giving up central power.

While people see decentralization as a panacea, there is a lack of understanding about why the process is important, about the challenges it would create, and about what kinds of services should be expected from the newly empowered municipal leaders. All of these discussions are taking place in an increasingly challenging security environment, placing additional pressure on the government to succeed.

Terrorist attacks in 2015 cut Tunisia's tourism revenue in half, and the sector has still not recovered with many local hotels along the beach sitting empty.

In March, the Tunisian military successfully fought off ISIS as it attempted to overtake a southern city along the Libyan border. And earlier this month, Tunisian security forces again foiled an ISIS plot, killing four, and arresting 16 others, and just last week took out another top leader of the Tunisian ISIS affiliate. These successes are encouraging, and they are evidence of the security sector's growing capacity, a development which should be welcomed by this administration.

The Tunisian security forces are proving themselves to be professional and capable partners that the United States can rely on to help fight extremism, to help push back against ISIS, and to assist other regional partners to face down the same threats. Tunisia is facing a dangerous and persistent terrorist threat from within and without, especially through the porous Libyan border, along the Algerian border, and from returning foreign fighters of which some estimates place at around 6,500 Tunisians. We need to be strengthening our security cooperation with Tunisia, including helping it to fight violent extremism, investing more in law enforcement through our INCLE programs, and assisting more with border security like we saw with the recent contract for equipment and training for a border surveillance system. So many of these security, political, and economic issues are intertwined and reinforcing of each other, that it is essential that the United States and Tunisia's international partners remain fully committed to Tunisia on all fronts.

I was disappointed to see the administration request almost $20 million less in FMF funds for Tunisia this year, funds for which there is a clear need and would go a long way toward helping Tunisia remain stable.

Similarly, I was disappointed to see only a modest request for ESF funds. There is a lot more that this administration can be doing, especially with technical assistance, helping making the structural reforms necessary to encourage investment and entrepreneurship, and with helping promote commerce, tourism, and trade with the United States and other partners.

Tunisia is ready and willing to accept our assistance, and there is no shortage of partners who stand ready and able to program any help that we can provide.

Tunisia is a country whose democratic, economic, and security successes are vital to our own interests. And despite the many challenges, it is overflowing with opportunity in an increasingly troubled region of the world. We cannot afford to be turning away, diverting our attention, or scaling back our engagement, and I encourage our administration to make Tunisia the priority that it warrants.

With that, I am so pleased to recognize the ranking member, my good friend, Congressman Ted Deutch of Florida.

Mr. DEUTCH. Thank you very much, Madam Chairman.

And thanks to our witnesses for appearing here today.

I know that this administration is committed to success of Tunisia, as are the members of this subcommittee. And I look forward to hearing how our policies and our systems are working toward that goal.

Five years have now passed since Tunisia's Jasmine revolution shook the region, and it's been clear that Tunisians want to see their nascent democracy thrive. Tunisia's leaders, while motivated in governing have difficult steps to take to undo decades of authoritarian rule. Unfortunately, slow progress has led to increasing disillusionment among Tunisians.

A region in turmoil has plunged this once relatively stable country into a security crisis that has affected its ability to bring about much needed economic growth. Youth unemployment is estimated to be over 30 percent, and the lack of job opportunities is frustrating Tunisia's young educated population, the very same demographic that drove the Jasmine Revolution.

In a recent poll, less than a third said that they believe the government is doing a good job addressing the country's problems. But hope is not lost, because the same poll found that 86 percent of Tunisians surveyed, still believes that democracy is the best form of governance.

Last week, Tunisia was granted nearly $8 billion in financing to help revise the economy, including a $2.8 billion 4-year emergency IMF loan, contingent on economic reforms to help increase employment opportunities and strengthen public institutions and a $5 billion World Bank loan to help bring about growth and create jobs.

The United States has invested heavily in bringing economic growth to Tunisia. The U.S.-Tunisia strategic dialogue most recently met in November 2015 and focused on economic opportunity, increasing trade, and strengthening partnerships and security cooperation.

I hope that we will see a follow-up meeting scheduled for this year. The Tunisia American Enterprise Fund aimed at bringing business and investments back to Tunisia has ceded $60 million since 2013. And the recent meeting of the U.S.-Tunisia joint economic commission has focused specifically on the ag or food sector, small and medium enterprises and information technology.

Unfortunately, an unstable security situation will not draw the new significant foreign investment that Tunisia badly needs. The horrific attacks on the Bardo Museum in Tunis and in Ben Guerdane have shaken Tunisian society and have dramatically decreased the foreign tourism that used to fuel the economy. The deteriorating situation in Libya, has had, and will continue to have, a dramatic impact on Tunisia as well.

Libya has served as home base to several of Tunisia's attackers. Tunisian forces, with the help of U.S. assistance, have stepped up efforts to control the border of Libya, and much of our assistance to Tunisia is now focused on counterterrorism.

If the decision is made for U.S. and coalition forces to go after ISIS in Libya, what effect will this have on Tunisia, which has so far sent a large contingent of foreign fighters to train with ISIS.

According to a recent Washington Post article, a strike in Libya killed 41 militants most of whom were Tunisians, just weeks before the attacks on Ben Guerdane. I am concerned that without greater prospects for employment, more young Tunisians will be drawn to ISIS' steady paycheck. And bringing about this kind of real change will take political will.

Thus far, Tunisia has faired well in transition of power with the country's leaders uniting for the good of the country. President Essebsi and his secular coalition joined with the Islamist Ennahda to form a unity government that has seen some moderate success in pushing through economic reforms, but progress on many other needed reforms has been slow.

In a recent surprising turn of events, last week, Ennahda announced the decision to separate religion from politics. As one media report put it, Ennahda's reform appear to try to distinguish itself in a region where political Islam has suffered setbacks. This, coupled with Tunisia's progressive by regional standards constitution bode well for the civility of the government.

The U.S. should continue to support programs that help improve good governance and streamline much of the bureaucracy left over from the Ben Ali era, and while I am heartened by this government's continued focus on transparency and accountability, I remain concerned about human rights abuses including those carried out by security forces. I also hope that we are using the voice of the United States Government to push for equal protection for the LGBT community, which has faced increasingly brutal persecution.

There are no shortage of challenges facing Tunisia, and we must be clear-eyed about the ability to successfully address them. But there at least seems to be willingness in the government to confront them, albeit slowly. And how can the U.S. most effectively support these reform efforts? How can we utilize our assistance to show the people of Tunisia that they should still have hope?

These are the questions that I look forward to discussing. I appreciate the administration's continued commitment to Tunisia, and I look forward to productive discussion today.

Thank you.

Ms. ROS-LEHTINEN. Thank you so much, Mr. Deutch.

Ms. Frankel.

Ms. FRANKEL. Madam Chair, I will wait until my turn.

Ms. ROS-LEHTINEN. Seeing no further request for time, it is my pleasure now to introduce our witnesses.

First, Mr. John Desrocher? Pretty good? Thank you. Who is deputy assistant secretary for Egypt and Maghreb Affairs for the State Department's Bureau of Near Eastern Affairs. Prior to this, he served as deputy chief of mission at the U.S. Embassy in Baghdad.

He has also served in New Zealand, Egypt, Israel, Liberia, and Germany. Welcome, Mr. Desrocher.

Next, we welcome Ms. Maria Longi. USAID's deputy assistant administrator for the Middle East. Prior to this, Ms. Longi served in various positions with the State Department and also worked at the millennium challenge cooperation as its director for threshold programs in several developing countries.

Welcome, Ms. Longi. We are pleased to have both of you here today. We thank you, both, for your service to our country. Your prepared statements will be made a part of the record.

And, Mr. Desrocher, we will begin with you.

STATEMENT OF MR. JOHN DESROCHER, DEPUTY ASSISTANT SECRETARY FOR EGYPT AND MAGHREB AFFAIRS, BUREAU OF NEAR EASTERN AFFAIRS, U.S. DEPARTMENT OF STATE

Mr. DESROCHER. Chairman Ros-Lehtinen, Ranking Member Deutch, members of the committee, I am honored to appear before you today to discuss our relations with the Republic of Tunisia.

It is a pleasure to share this table with my talented friend and colleague, Maria Longi, USAID's deputy assistant administrator for the Middle East.

Tunisia's 2011 revolution sparked the Arab Spring or Arab Awakening, which continues to reverberate throughout the region. While other countries have struggled with their transitions, Tunisia has emerged with a nascent yet stable democratic government. Tunisians have a constitution widely hailed as one of the most progressive in the Middle East, and they have conducted two sets of transparent and credible elections.

I am happy to report that the Tunisian-American partnership continues to deepen and mature as we confront shared security challenges, build sustainable economic growth that benefits both nations, and build strong democratic inclusive tradition that serves as a model for the region.

Tunisia is a reliable partner, and we can make it stronger if we continue to show our support.

Tunisia continues to face considerable challenges. Between 3,000 and 6,000 Tunisians have joined extremist groups abroad, and the horrific attacks of 2015 underline the very real threat that extremists pose to Tunisia. We cannot address security challenges in Tunisia without discussing Libyan instability. The attackers in the Bardo and Sousse attacks received training in Libyan terrorist camps, and there are between 250,000 and 1 million Libyans currently displaced from their own country and living in Tunisia. Without a permanent political solution to the ongoing strife in Libya, Tunisia will continue to face real and persistent security challenges from across the border.

Our assistance funding is helping the Tunisian security services develop a more agile security forces that respect human rights and democratic principles. Tunisia has used the United States as a principal partner in its efforts to strengthen military and civil police authorities. Our support will enhance security forces' capacity to counter threats from internal and external groups, monitor Tunisia's borders, communicate, and coordinate internally more effectively, and combat terrorists in diverse environments.

Our support also helps the civilian criminal justice sector improve respect for the rule of law and promote citizens security and access to justice across Tunisia.

Additionally, in 2015, President Obama designated Tunisia a major non-NATO ally in recognition of our shared values and Tunisia's strategic importance as a democratic success and critical line of defense against instability.

Tunisia continues to develop long neglected government institutions, or practices of the old regime linger. We are concerned about reports of corruption at all levels of government. Tunisia's big 10 government moves slowly. The ongoing disputes in the key party of the governing coalition has slowed decision further and reforms do not come as quickly as we would like.

But Tunisian officials rightly take pride in their country's exemplary efforts to promote the rule of law, transparency, and accountability, reform its security sector, and reinforce principles of democratic governance. Tunisians across the spectrum of society recognize that human rights abuses and corruption must be addressed and actively seek ways to create change. In recognition of the important role of civil society in advancing reform, Tunisia has joined the open government partnership and is partnering with civil society to promote transparency, accountability and participation in government.

Senior government officials are working to address challenges and repeatedly voice their commitment to reform.

More needs to be done on all of these fronts, but establishing transparency and accountability mechanisms and a culture of zero tolerance of corruption will take time.

Tunisia's faltering economy compounds the challenges facing the Tunisian Government. GDP growth in 2015 was anemic at 0.08 percent. Last year's terrorist attacks devastated the tourism industry, unemployment is over 15 percent, and twice as high as that for recent graduates, those living in the interior of the country, and for women.

Despite these difficulties, the Tunisian Government has made meaningful progress on economic reforms. They have already passed public-private partnership, bankruptcy, and banking laws, among others. I am optimistic that Tunisians will pass the new investment code this summer. Such reforms are laying the groundwork for increased investment trade and private sector engagement between the United States and Tunisia.

As Tunisians move forward on reforms to take steps to provide economic opportunity, they are holding fast to their democratic ideals. The full range of political actors, including political Islamists, are working together constructively to build Tunisia's democratic traditions.

Our investments in Tunisia have been rewarded by the steady development of inclusive governance institutions and processes, increased stability and security, and great strides toward financial sustainability. As a strategic partner and powerful example of a successful Arab democracy, Tunisians still need and want our support.

The development of a fully functioning and transparent democracy will take time and patience as Tunisians' leaders strengthen their institutions. With the help of Congress and our interagency colleagues, we will continue our work to build an even stronger partner in a volatile region.

I want to thank you, again, for the opportunity to testify, and I look forward to answering any questions you might have. Thank you very much.

[The prepared statement of Mr. Desrocher follows:]

Statement for the Record
John Desrocher, Deputy Assistant Secretary of State for Near Eastern Affairs

House Foreign Affairs Committee
Subcommittee on the Middle East and North Africa
May 25, 2016

Chairman Ros-Lehtinen, Ranking Member Deutch, and Members of the Committee, I am honored to appear before you today to discuss our relations with the Republic of Tunisia. It is a pleasure to share this panel with my talented friend and colleague Maria Longi, USAID's Deputy Assistant Administrator to the Middle East. Together, our institutions, along with others in the executive branch, are working to help Tunisia's government and people develop their economy, face the menace of violent extremism, and develop their democratic institutions and rule of law.

Tunisia's 2011 revolution sparked the Arab Spring, or Arab Awakening, which continues to reverberate throughout the region. While other countries have struggled with their transitions, Tunisia has emerged with a nascent yet stable democratic government. They have a constitution widely hailed as one of the most progressive in the Middle East, and they have conducted two sets of transparent and credible elections.

I am happy to report that the Tunisian-American partnership continues to deepen and mature as we confront shared security challenges, build sustainable economic growth that benefits both nations, and build a strong democratic, inclusive tradition that serves as a model for the region. Tunisia is a reliable partner, and we can make it stronger if we continue to show our support through its transition.

Tunisia continues to face considerable challenges. Between 3,000 and 6,000 Tunisians have joined extremist groups abroad--especially in Libya--placing Tunisia among the largest per-capita source countries of foreign terrorist fighters in the world. While this bolsters the ranks of those seeking to destabilize the region, it also poses a long-term challenge to Tunisia as those extremists return. The horrific attacks of 2015 – at the Bardo Museum in March, on the beach in Sousse in June, and again in downtown Tunis in November – underline the very real threat that extremists pose to Tunisia. The March 7, 2016 attack on Ben Guerdane, in which nearly 100 Da'esh-affiliated attackers crossed the border and sought to overwhelm security forces and take control of the city, also accentuated the danger that instability in neighboring Libya poses to Tunisian security. In that case, the Tunisian military heroically and professionally thwarted the attack.

We cannot address security challenges in Tunisia without discussing Libya. Instability in Libya is a threat to Tunisian national security, which was evident even before Ben Guerdane. The attackers in the Bardo and Sousse attacks received training in Libyan terrorist camps. Between 250,000 and 1 million Libyans currently live in Tunisia, having fled instability in their own country, which strains communities' capacity to serve their citizens' needs. We must have a viable Government of National Accord in Libya as it works to establish peace and security, and as a partner to counter the threat Da'esh poses to the region and beyond. Without a permanent political solution to the ongoing strife in Libya, Tunisia will continue to face real and persistent security challenges from across the border.

Tunisian security forces continue build capacity to respond to threats and prevent violence. Our assistance funding is helping the Tunisian security services develop a more agile force that respects human rights and democratic principles. Increased law enforcement and intelligence work and cooperation with partners are important steps to maintain security. Tunisia views the United States as a principal partner in its efforts to strengthen military and civil police authorities. In 2014, President Obama named Tunisia as one of six countries to participate in the Security Governance Initiative, aimed at supporting partner governments to develop sound policies, institutional structures, systems, and processes to deliver security and justice to their citizens. Our support will enhance security forces' capacity to counter increasing threats from internal and external groups, monitor Tunisia's borders, communicate and coordinate internally more effectively, and combat terrorists in diverse environments. Our support also helps the civilian criminal justice sector improve respect for the rule of law and promote citizen security and access to justice across Tunisia. We note the response of the Tunisian security forces to the Ben Guerdane attack, and the restrained peacekeeping efforts of civil police during recent economic protests. These events show that our long-term investment to help train Tunisia's civilian security forces is paying dividends. We will continue to build upon this success in the future.

Another important element of our approach to supporting Tunisian security needs is our Trans-Sahara Counterterrorism Partnership (TSCTP). It uses a whole-of-government approach in the Maghreb and the Sahel to build capacity and promote regional cooperation and coordination. The Department of State, USAID, and Department of Defense work together with our Tunisian partners to design and implement counterterrorism and countering violent extremism (CVE) and security sector reform measures. The TSCTP coordination mechanism has provided a platform for sharing best practices and lessons learned, including models for monitoring and evaluating the return on investment for programs.

Additionally, in 2015, President Obama designated Tunisia a Major Non-NATO Ally in recognition of our shared values and Tunisia's strategic importance as a democratic success and critical line of defense against instability from neighboring Libya. Major Non-NATO Ally status comes with tangible privileges including eligibility for training, loans of equipment for cooperative research and development, and Foreign Military Financing for commercial leasing of certain defense articles.

Tunisia continues to develop long-neglected government institutions, but practices of the old regime linger. I note reports from human rights groups that repressive practices continue by some members of Tunisia's security forces. We are also concerned about reports of corruption at all levels of government that reflect the economic hardship faced by many Tunisians, the oversaturation of government payrolls, and the culture of permissiveness that built over the Ben Ali era. Tunisia's big tent government moves slowly. The ongoing upheaval in a key party of the governing coalition has slowed decision-making further, and reforms do not come as quickly as we would like. This is a challenge that will surely be surmounted, hopefully drawing on the same democratic values that have imbued Tunisia's Arab Spring.

But Tunisia is confronting these political challenges. Tunisian officials rightly take pride in their country's exemplary efforts to promote rule of law, transparency, and accountability; reform its security sector; and reinforce principles of democratic governance. Tunisians across the spectrum of society recognize that human rights abuse and corruption must be addressed, and actively seek ways to create change. Tunisia's civil society is more vigorous and vocal than ever before, and parliament-watchers, civil rights advocates, and minority rights activists feed into an open media dialogue about the democratic values Tunisians hold dear. In recognition of the important role of civil society in advancing reform, Tunisia has joined the Open Government Partnership and is partnering with civil society to promote transparency, accountability, and participation in government. Senior government officials are working to address challenges and repeatedly voice their commitment to reform. The Ministers of Interior and Justice have spoken out against prisoner abuse and held security officials accountable. Tunisia also recently created a ministry specifically focused on combatting corruption. More needs to be done on all these fronts, but establishing transparency and accountability mechanisms and a culture of zero tolerance of corruption will take time.

Tunisia's faltering economy compounds the challenges facing the Tunisian government. GDP growth in 2015 was anemic at 0.8 percent. The Tunisians hope to get back to 2 percent growth this year, but even this figure is significantly below the 10-year average of 5.7 percent growth before the 2011 revolution. Last year's terrorist attacks devastated the tourism industry, which accounts for 12 percent of GDP and which, even before the two attacks, remained below pre-revolution levels. Unemployment is over 15 percent, and twice as high for recent graduates, those living in the interior of the country, and women. Tunisia needs to generate about 100,000 jobs every year to keep pace with the projected growth of the workforce, particularly university graduates. Tunisia's fiscal deficit increased from 0.6 percent of GDP in 2010 to 4.1 percent of GDP in 2014. The government is seeking to balance influential private sector interests with powerful labor unions as it seeks to open up the economy to greater competition, expanded entrepreneurship and modern business practices, which is the path to higher growth.

Despite the difficult economy, the Tunisian government has made meaningful progress on economic reforms. They have already passed Public Private Partnership, Banking and Bankruptcy laws, among others. I am optimistic the Tunisians will get a new investment code passed this summer. As Secretary of Commerce Penny Pritzker has noted, "Tunisia must streamline, simplify, and clarify its complicated investment code – to send a signal to local and global investors that Tunisia is open for business." In the recent Joint Economic Commission (JEC), we also worked closely with the government and private sector to address sub-national reforms that will increase access to finance, connect more Tunisians to the internet, and build trade linkages for their agricultural sector that benefit both countries. Such reforms are laying the groundwork for increased investment, trade, and private sector engagement between the United States and Tunisia. Moreover, these reforms expand Tunisia's openness to new business activity and international investment. We look forward to building on the commitments of the JEC over the coming year, and continue looking for opportunities to promote private sector growth and public sector cooperation.

As Tunisians move forward on reforms and take steps to provide economic opportunity they are holding fast to their democratic ideals. The full range of political actors, including political Islamists, are working together constructively to build Tunisia's democratic traditions. Our investments in Tunisia have been rewarded by the steady development of inclusive governance institutions and processes, increased stability and security, and great strides toward financial sustainability. As a strategic partner and powerful example of a successful Arab democracy working together to move forward, Tunisians still need--and want--our support.

The development of a fully functioning and transparent democracy will take time and patience as Tunisia's leaders strengthen their institutions and work to ensure the freedoms guaranteed to Tunisian citizens by their constitution. With the help of Congress and our interagency colleagues, we will continue our work to build an even stronger partner in a volatile region.

I want to thank you, again, for the opportunity to testify and I look forward to answering any questions you have. Thank you.

Ms. ROS-LEHTINEN. Thank you so much, Mr. Desrocher.
And now we will turn to Ms. Longi.

STATEMENT OF MS. MARIA LONGI, DEPUTY ASSISTANT ADMINISTRATOR, BUREAU FOR THE MIDDLE EAST, U.S. AGENCY FOR INTERNATIONAL DEVELOPMENT

Ms. LONGI. Thank you.

Chairman Ros-Lehtinen, Ranking Member Deutch, and members of the subcommittee, thank you for the opportunity to discuss U.S. assistance to Tunisia and our partnership with the Tunisian people as they work for a stable democracy and economic prosperity.

We agree with Chairman Royce's recent assertion that Tunisia represents hope for democracy, peace, and security in the Middle East and North Africa. U.S. assistance serves as an important demonstration of our commitment to Tunisians as they work to consolidate reforms. We recognize that the 2011 revolution was sparked by the Tunisian people's frustrations with the stifling of political discourse, a corrupt economic environment, and a predatory security apparatus.

I would like to talk briefly about how the U.S. Government quickly and effectively responded to support Tunisia's aspirations for change, describe what we are doing in Tunisia today, and outline how we plan to scale up our support for the democratic transition and economic reforms.

Since 2011, USAID has provided approximately $300 million to support Tunisia's economic growth and democratic transition. This includes two sovereign loan guarantees that provided access to $985 million in financing, and helped support Tunisia's efforts to reform and grow its economy.

In the fall of 2011, the United States provided assistance to organizations in Tunisia that were organizing and administering multiparty elections for a Constituent Assembly charged with drafting a new constitution. Among our activities, we were able to connect U.S. Supreme Court Justices Stephen Breyer and Ruth Bader Ginsburg with members of the Constituent Assembly, political party representatives, and Tunisian legal scholars. This and other real practical engagements with emerging Tunisian leaders and civil society immediately after the revolution helped us to identify areas we could help going forward.

Another major area of U.S. engagement in Tunisia centers around its struggling economy. Through careful analysis, we identified significant constraints to job creation and economic growth in Tunisia, which we are working to address in many ways, including helping Tunisian firms unlock opportunities for growth and supporting job creation, training young entrepreneurs in marginalized areas, and providing technical assistance to Tunisia's Government as it drafts and implements laws to improve the investment climate and encourage private sector development.

These efforts have the immediate benefit of educating and employing Tunisia's youth to ensure a better future for them. As an example of how our work is directly responding to the needs of aspiring Tunisian workers, I would like to highlight a program for training Tunisian entrepreneurs in marginalized areas, primarily those close to Tunisia's borders with Algeria and Libya. This is a partnership with Hewlett Packard, the United Nation's Industrial Development Organization, and the Government of Italy, where USAID leveraged our resources to bring online entrepreneurship training for 12,000 Tunisians. More than 1,600 Tunisians have found new employment through this activity.

Among these entrepreneurs is Anis Assali, a young man who spent 14 months unable to find a job in the capital, Tunis, after earning a degree in aerospace engineering from the University of Tunis. He returned to his hometown in western Tunisia and decided to create his own employment by starting a business selling and installing solar panels. USAID-backed programs supported him with training and marketing and identifying reliable partners. His business has now grown from solar electricity to include solar water heating.

Another USAID program is working with businesses like Nozha Dates, based 300 miles southwest of Tunis. Nozha traditionally sold to an export company that wanted to develop direct export capabilities. USAID helped the company improve its standards, which enabled it to hire 55 new employees for its direct export business. All in all, USAID's programs in Tunisia have helped create more than 14,000 new jobs in 2 years alone and we are on track to create even more jobs by this time next year.

Thanks to the support of Congress, USAID's assistance is addressing targeted areas where U.S. and Tunisian partnerships can have the most impact. Our economic growth activities will continue to focus on employment through a firm level approach that helps firms identify and overcome internal blockages to growth, while also working with the Government of Tunisia to reform critical policies, regulations, and processes to limit the competitiveness of Tunisian businesses.

The U.S. will work to strengthen local governance capacity, placing a special emphasis on marginalized communities and underserved governorates and localities. Our programs will aim to provide citizens groups and civil society organizations with advocacy and outreach skills to articulate community priorities.

Right now, we have highly skilled technical teams in Tunisia consulting with key stakeholders to design targeted and strategic programs that will support Tunisia's democratic and economic transition. As we know well, the transition to a more democratic society and a more open and inclusive economic environment can be rocky and can move at intermittent speeds. Tunisia has made impressive strides in the past 5 years, and we recognize that there are a still long way to go.

With the support of Congress, USAID hopes to do even more to partner with Tunisia in its transition, working hand in hand with the Tunisian people to fulfill their aspirations. A successful Tunisia benefits the Tunisian people, the region, and the United States.

Thank you, and I look forward to your questions.

[The prepared statement of Ms. Longi follows:]

Statement of Maria Longi
Deputy Assistant Administrator, Bureau for the Middle East
U.S. Agency for International Development
House Committee on Foreign Affairs
Middle East and North Africa Subcommittee

"Tunisia's Struggle for Stability, Security, and Democracy"
May 25, 2016

Chairman Ros-Lehtinen, Ranking Member Deutch, and Members of the Subcommittee, thank you for the opportunity to discuss U.S. assistance to Tunisia and our partnership with the Tunisian people as they work to foster a stable democracy and economic prosperity.

Tunisia remains a high priority for the United States. We agree with Chairman Royce's recent assertion that Tunisia represents hope for democracy, peace and security in the Middle East and North Africa. Tunisia is the only country from the 2011 Arab Awakening that has successfully realized a peaceful path to democracy. U.S. assistance serves as an important demonstration of our commitment to the people of Tunisia as they work to consolidate democratic reforms that will support inclusive economic and social opportunity.

We recognize that the Jasmine Revolution was sparked by the Tunisian people's frustration with the stifling of political discourse, a corrupt economic environment, and predatory security apparatus that coalesced to strip the dignity of citizens. As the U.S. Agency for International Development (USAID) says in our mission statement, we seek to partner with Tunisia to end extreme poverty and promote a resilient, democratic society while advancing our security and prosperity. I'd like to talk briefly about how the U.S. government quickly and effectively responded to support Tunisians' aspirations for change, describe what we are doing in Tunisia today, and outline how we plan to scale up our support for the democratic transition and economic reforms.

Immediate post-revolution support
Since 2011, USAID has provided approximately $300 million to support Tunisia's economic growth and democratic transition. This includes two sovereign loan guarantees that provided Tunisia with access to $985 million in financing and helped support Tunisia's efforts to reform and grow its economy.

In the fall of 2011, the United States provided assistance to organizations in Tunisia that were organizing and administering multiparty elections for a Constituent Assembly charged with drafting a new constitution. We also sponsored a constitutional development program that connected two U.S. Supreme Court justices with members of the Constituent Assembly, political party representatives and Tunisian legal scholars. This assistance helped inform the underlying architecture for Tunisia's new government, including safeguards for an independent judiciary, the separation of powers, and religious liberty.

Our real, practical engagements with emerging Tunisian leaders and civil society immediately after the revolution helped us to identify areas we could help going forward.

Current programming
Through careful analysis, we identified significant constraints to job creation and economic growth in Tunisia, highlighting the non-functional labor code and poor business enabling environment. With more than $1.4 billion in annual trade between our countries, we already have an important economic relationship. USAID has been working to address constraints to job creation and economic growth in many ways, including helping Tunisian firms unlock opportunities for growth and supporting job creation, training young entrepreneurs in marginalized areas, and providing technical assistance to Tunisia's government as it drafts and implements laws to improve the investment climate and encourage private sector development. These efforts have the immediate benefit of educating and employing Tunisia's youth to ensure a better future for them, as well as fostering a stable, prosperous democracy, benefitting the region and the United States.

At the strategic level, USAID has embedded technical advisors in the Ministry of Finance, working with the Minister and strategic directorates within the Ministry to provide advice and best practices on tax and customs reforms and implementation, which will improve the environment for U.S. and Tunisian companies to do business together. This ongoing work also complements assistance provided from the Department of the Treasury to the Central Bank and Ministry of Finance. The Minister has repeatedly remarked on the critical support that our advisors have provided and their vital role in helping his Ministry drive important reforms to improve the business and investment climate.

Our current support also includes the Tunisian-American Enterprise Fund, which has already invested $60 million in Tunisian small and medium enterprises. Other assistance activities support young Tunisian entrepreneurs launch start-ups, job creation, and employability programs. Our assistance also extends to the Tunisian government in the area of revenue generation and free market reforms. Additionally, we are finalizing the negotiations with the Government of Tunisia for a third sovereign loan guarantee for up to $500 million.

As an example of how our work is directly responding to the needs of aspiring Tunisian workers, I would like to highlight our training of Tunisian entrepreneurs in marginalized areas, primarily those close to Tunisia's borders with Algeria and Libya. This is a partnership with Hewlett Packard, the United Nations Industrial Development Organization (UNIDO), and the Government of Italy, where USAID leveraged our resources to bring online entrepreneurship training to 12,000 Tunisians. More than 1,600 Tunisians have found new employment through this activity.

Among these entrepreneurs is Anis Assali. Anis is a young man who spent 14 months unable to find a job in the capital, Tunis, after earning a degree in aerospace engineering from the University of Tunis. He returned to his hometown of Le Kef, in western Tunisia, and decided to create his own employment by starting a business selling and installing solar panels. The USAID-backed program supported him with training in marketing and identifying reliable suppliers. His business has now grown from solar electricity to include solar water heating, and the USAID-supported program has helped connect Anis with a global community of like-minded "green business" entrepreneurs.

Another USAID program, the Business Reform and Competitiveness Project, is working with businesses like Nozha Dates, which is based in the economically disadvantaged region of Tozeur, nearly 300 miles southwest of Tunis. Nozha traditionally sold to an export company, but wanted to develop its own labeling and direct export capabilities. The USAID program helped the company meet export standards and work through regulations. This enabled Nozha Dates to hire 55 new employees to handle logistics, production, processing and quality management for its direct export business.

All in all, USAID programs in Tunisia have helped create more than 12,000 new, sustainable, private-sector jobs in the past two years. We are on track to create even more jobs by this time next year. We have also worked with the Tunisian government to match job seekers with firms looking to hire, and also to ensure that young people are educated and trained to match the needs of modern private-sector businesses. USAID works with multiple ministries to connect higher education institutions with local private sector firms and align curricula more closely with local labor demands. The Tunisian government is using USAID-supported career centers as one of the pillars of national education reform, and exploring options to expand the model across the country.

Going Forward

Thanks to the support of Congress, USAID's assistance is addressing targeted areas where U.S. and Tunisian partnerships can have the most impact. This increase reflects the U.S. Government's commitment to expanding economic and governance partnerships between the United States and Tunisia, and the important reforms that Tunisia is putting in place, on issues such as corporate and personal income taxation, and data privacy.

Our economic growth activities will continue to focus on employment through a firm-level approach that helps firms identify and overcome internal blockages to growth, while also working with the Government of Tunisia to reform critical policies, regulations and processes that limit the competitiveness of Tunisian businesses. These efforts, together with the enterprise fund and other donor inputs, have made significant strides in contributing to inclusive economic growth and employment in Tunisia.

In response to a Tunisian government request and in order to closely target our assistance to the government's priorities and our comparative advantage, we are now finalizing a Country Development Cooperation Strategy for Tunisia. This strategy, which guides USAID's long-term engagement in country with input from a variety of stakeholders, focuses on economic opportunity and private sector growth to create much needed jobs, as well as improve the participation of marginalized communities in local governance, strengthen community resilience in areas most vulnerable to violent extremist ideology, and improve the government's responsiveness to citizen needs.

To promote fair and open decisions on budgetary allocation of resources to support the decentralization process, we will also work with the government to improve the transparency, accountability and inclusivity of the government's public financial management system.

The U.S. will work to strengthen local governance capacity, placing a special emphasis on marginalized communities in underserved governorates and localities. Our programs will aim to provide citizens' groups and civil society organizations with advocacy and outreach skills to articulate community priorities, while supporting local government to implement participatory systems and to follow through on local election pledges and mandates.

Right now, we have highly-skilled technical teams in Tunisia consulting with key stakeholders from the Tunisian government, private sector, and civil society to design targeted and strategic programs that will support Tunisia's democratic and economic transition.

In addition, USAID is participating in the Security Governance Initiative (SGI) in Tunisia having served on both consultation visits and helping define the objectives and activities for the Joint Country Action Plan. This initiative is an innovative, multi-year partnership between the United States and African nations that offers targeted approaches to improving security sector governance and capacity. SGI's central objective is to support partner governments to develop sound policies, institutional structures, systems, and processes to more efficiently, effectively, and responsibly deliver security and justice to their citizens. It is encouraging to see an initiative focused on utilizing U.S. government expertise to address not only security issues, but governance issues as well.

It is important to note that while USAID is conducting its own careful analysis of needs, we are also working to respond to Tunisian-identified priorities. The citizens and government of Tunisia know their challenges better than anyone, and they have been honest and direct about the road ahead and the steps needed to maintain the momentum of the 2011 revolution.

Conclusion
As we know well, the transition to a more open democratic society, and a more open and inclusive economic environment, can be rocky and move at intermittent speeds.

Tunisia has made impressive strides in the past five years, and we recognize that there is still a long way to go. With the support of Congress, USAID hopes to do even more to support Tunisia during its democratic and economic transition, working hand in hand with the Tunisian people to fulfill their aspirations. A successful Tunisia benefits the Tunisian people, the region, and the United States.

Thank you for giving me the opportunity to testify, and I look forward to your questions.

Ms. Ros-Lehtinen. Thank you very much for great testimony.

We will begin the question-and-answer period.

As both of you have stated, seeing Tunisia's democratic transition through is critical to U.S. interests and regional stability. But because of a modest budget request and other issues vying for attention, it may appear as though the administration doesn't view Tunisia as one of its top priorities.

While the administration's Fiscal Year 2017 request for Tunisia represents a slight increase over the prior years, the ESF request is for $74 million, $20 million of which is for the Enterprise Fund, and the FMF request is $45 million, which is $20 million less than last year.

So many of the challenges in Tunisia are interdependent, and I fear that what will happen if the government can't show the people that it can provide security while simultaneously growing the economy and expanding political inclusion could be a recipe for disaster.

So I ask, why aren't we doing more to promote democracy and governance and to contribute to the country's badly needed economic growth? Why was the FMF request for Tunisia reduced for the upcoming fiscal year? And what is the status of military equipment requested by Tunisia? Is there anything being held up?

Mr. Desrocher. Thank you very much for your question.

Obviously, we are and remain extremely supportive and this administration is very supportive of Tunisia and Tunisian's efforts to build their democracy. And we have a robust interaction across many areas. Obviously, the assistance programs that we have talked about, but it goes beyond assistance to our governmental interactions and our interactions with the private sector.

We, of course, President Caid Essebsi was here last year to see President Obama, and Secretary Kerry was in Tunisia last fall for the strategic dialogue. We also have the joint economic committee, which has done a great deal to address the barriers to interactions and trade between our two private sectors. We have a joint military commission that deals with our military assistance issues, and we recently had very useful trade and investment framework agreement discussions about trade issues particularly in Tunisia.

On the assistance side, we have crafted our assistance program very carefully. We think it meets the requirements that Tunisia has. We think it is robust, and we will continue to have a robust program going forward.

We are moving forward with our military assistance across a broad range of areas designed to increase Tunisian security services' mobility, their surveillance capabilities, their border security capabilities, and we think that is very successful. We are moving forward on different aspects of military assistance very well and feel very positive about that. And we also have, you know, robust ESF programs that Maria has outlined, and you know, we feel confident that we have built an assistance program for Tunisia that matches its needs.

Ms. Ros-Lehtinen. Thank you.

Ms. Longi. I will also say that the increase that we saw in Fiscal Year 2016 has prompted us to go out and design some really robust and new democracy programs. And so as I have mentioned, our teams are in the field right now designing those, and they will address some of the issues that you raised, Chairman, on the local governance and the decentralization and the empowerment of youth.

And so we are excited to get those designs completed and entrained, and I guess time will tell how much more we can absorb on that front. But we are moving forward robustly on expanding.

Ms. ROS-LEHTINEN. Thank you to both.

On the Tunisian American Enterprise Fund, it was established to respond to an urgent need for investment and job creation in Tunisia, but there is some questions surrounding its effectiveness.

How many projects has the Enterprise Fund implemented so far? How many jobs has it helped to create? And what barometers do you use to measure the success of the fund?

Ms. LONGI. Yes. So the Enterprise Fund was created almost 3 years ago, and they did make their first investments about, almost 2 years in, which is—from what I understand, it is pretty commensurate with prior investment funds. They did have to figure out how to work in the complex legal and regulatory environment, which is as we have mentioned is changing and improving. So that was part of their start.

They have invested about $10 million to date in about five or six companies, and our most recent discussions with the fund tells us that they have about $45 million in projects that they are doing due diligence on right now, and they have told us that those are very, very promising projects. And so we expect to see a lot more investments this year and next as they get through the due diligence.

I think as far as what would be successful, the goal of the Enterprise Fund is to create a robust private sector and help the SME sector and on lending to micro finance. And so as they make more investments, those will be the types of things that we are monitoring. I am not clear yet on the jobs created. We can go back and bring you some information on that. I would assume that it is probably not too high yet with the five companies, but we can get back to you on that one.

[The information referred to follows:]

WRITTEN RESPONSE RECEIVED FROM MS. MARIA LONGI TO QUESTION ASKED DURING THE HEARING BY THE HONORABLE ILEANA ROS-LEHTINEN

According to TAEF's Monitoring and Evaluation annual report, in calendar year 2015 TAEF created 524 jobs.

Ms. ROS-LEHTINEN. Thank you very much. And I also would like to point out that we have the Tunisian Ambassador to the United States with us, a good friend of this subcommittee.

Welcome, sir.

And with that, I am very pleased to yield to my good friend, Mr. Deutch, for his time.

Mr. DEUTCH. Thanks, Madam Chair.

Mr. Desrocher, last week the head of Ennahda said we are leaving political Islam to enter Muslim democracy. We are Muslim democrats who no longer claim political Islam. Two questions. One, what are the implications for Tunisian democracy? And, two, does the statement have broader implications for the future of political Islam in the Middle East?

Mr. DESROCHER. Thank you very much for the question.

Regarding Ennahda, the Ennahda party has played a very constructive role in the development of Tunisia's democracy since the revolution in 2011. They have played actively in the political sphere consistently, continuously since then. They have worked well with the rest of the Tunisian leadership in this very consensus-based approach that Tunisian leaders have taken to building their democracy. We think that is very laudable. Ennahda stepped back, last year, during a difficult period in Tunisia in favor of a caretaker government in advance of the national elections that were held last fall. Ennahda participated in those and is in Parliament and is also in the current cabinet and continues to participate very constructively.

As far as the announcements that you mentioned, you know, as you noted and as the leadership of Ennahda has said publicly, they are taking the step to draw distinction between political activities and between, you know, religious and cultural and civic activities.

What that will mean in practice I think that, you know, we will see going forward. But, certainly, Ennahda's track record suggests that they have up until now and we certainly, you know, think they will continue to play a very—make a very productive and useful contribution to the building of Tunisian's democracy.

Mr. DEUTCH. Thank you. And, Mr. Desrocher, just to stick with you for a second, homosexuality remains a crime in Tunisia, punishable by up to 3 years in prison. Some LGBT defenders have accused the police of being complicit in crimes against the community. This is seemingly in congress with Tunisia's values of pluralism and tolerance. And I just wonder whether this intolerance might alienate potential investors, whether it might challenge Tunisia's economic recovery?

Mr. DESROCHER. That is something that concerns us as well. For many reasons, including, as you say, you know, it is not consistent with Tunisia's desire to create a welcoming environment for the investment that it so badly needs. This is a topic that we are in continuous contact with Tunisian counterparts about and also with Tunisians themselves. Our Embassy is in regular touch with advocacy groups that are concerned about these issues and it is something that we are concerned about and that we address with our Tunisian counterparts at every opportunity.

Mr. DEUTCH. Great. I appreciate that.

Ms. Longi, I was struck, and I think perhaps a lot of us don't think enough about the Libyan refugee issue. The number is somewhere between, I think ¼ million and up to 1 million displaced Libyans in Tunisia. What is being done to assist them? How does the government—I guess this is for both of you. But has the government approached this issue and what impact does it have on economic growth within Tunisia?

Ms. LONGI. USAID has not addressed the Libyan refugee issue specifically, and so I am going to punt.

Mr. DESROCHER. Certainly. You know, the influx of Libyans into Tunisia has certainly put a strain on, you know, the availability of housing, the Tunisian medical system, and so on, which I have to say, Tunisians have reacted extraordinarily admirably and supportively to this influx of refugees from Libya.

But it is something that is causing a strain. And really, you know, what, of course, we really need to do is redouble our efforts with Libyans, with our partners in the international community, to strengthen a unity government in Libya and to restore some stability there so that, you know, Tunisia is not put in the position of having to host this really considerable number of people.

Mr. DEUTCH. All right. Thank you, both.

I yield back my time.

Ms. ROS-LEHTINEN. Thank you so much, Mr. Deutch.

Mr. Weber of Texas.

Mr. WEBER. Thank you, Madam Chair.

Gosh, I am learning some things about Tunisia here today. The population of Tunisia, I guess, is only——

Mr. DESROCHER. About 11 million.

Mr. WEBER. About 11 million. How many square miles?

Mr. DESROCHER. I am sorry. I am not real good at that kind of geography. Sorry.

Mr. WEBER. Okay. But it can't be bigger than Texas, right? Nothing is bigger——

Mr. DESROCHER. No. For the record, nothing is bigger than Texas.

Mr. WEBER. I just want to make sure. So according to my notes, President Obama designated it as a major non-NATO ally. How many major, or non-NATO allies do we currently have? Do you know?

Mr. DESROCHER. I would have to go back to be certain. I think it is—boy, you know, instead of speculating, I will go back and check. It is in the realm of a dozen or so, perhaps, slightly more. But let me get back to you.

Mr. WEBER. So how many NATO allies?

Mr. DESROCHER. 28 members of NATO.

Mr. WEBER. So 28 members of NATO, and we have about—and we have designated about—or the President has, or at least at this point there is a dozen non-NATO allies?

Mr. DESROCHER. Let me get back and make sure I know the numbers there, because they are spread all over the world.

Mr. WEBER. Okay. So I notice we are doing some things. We are helping them with arms sales. How do we make sure the arms don't fall into the wrong—one of you said, and I don't want to put words—there was 3,000 to 6,000 Tunisians joined extremist groups? Is that right?

Mr. DESROCHER. The estimate is that roughly that number have left Tunisia to join Daesh and other extremist groups primarily in Iraq and Syria.

Mr. WEBER. Is that from 2011 on?

Mr. DESROCHER. Yeah. That would be over the past years. Yes, that is right.

Mr. WEBER. Okay. But starting with the quote/unquote——

Mr. DESROCHER. Yes. Yes.

Mr. WEBER. Okay. You said there are 11 million. So 6,000—3,000 to 6,000 have joined.

How are we making sure that the arms that we are helping Tunisia with don't fall into the wrong hands?

Mr. DESROCHER. Well, we have got, you know, very robust and close relations with our compatriots—with our counterparts, I should say, in the Tunisian security sector. And we are helping with lots of training. We are helping with material, particularly that helps in regards as far as mobility and border security and surveillance and so on.

And generally, as a rule, these foreign fighters are leaving the country in dribs and drabs through commercial means by various routes to get to Iraq and Syria. Meaning they are not really in a position to take things with them unfortunately.

Mr. WEBER. Which leads me to my next—is it—how do you say your name? Is it——

Mr. DESROCHER. Desrocher.

Mr. WEBER. Desrocher. Mr. Desrocher, are any of the political leaders leaving the country? Are they identifiable as part of the that 3,000 to 6,000 route? Any notable defections so to speak?

Mr. DESROCHER. No. No. Not at all. These are young men, you know, generally from pretty challenged backgrounds who, you know, as I think a couple of the speakers have noted today, have been pulled in by some of this propaganda that we all see regarding ISIL and its goals. But this is—no, it is not a leadership issue in that sense.

Mr. WEBER. Okay. And then, is it Longi? Is that how you say that?

Ms. LONGI. Longi.

Mr. WEBER. Ms. Longi, you said earlier that your team is going out to design, and I think I am quoting you now, real robust democracy programs or something to that effect. How do you define a real robust democracy program? Tell us about that.

Ms. LONGI. Well, with the increased funding that we received in Fiscal Year 2016, real and robust. So we are looking at the needs on the ground and consulting with stakeholders. The areas where we are most likely to engage are on the decentralization in the local government, reforms that were enshrined in the new constitution. And so we are going to be collaborating with the World Bank, part of the World Bank program that was reference earlier. We will do work in this area and we will try to plug in where we can have an impact there.

Some of the other areas where we will work is with these new and stronger local governments, working with them on public financial management so——

Mr. WEBER. Forgive the interruption. But when you say new local governments, states, counties, cities? How do you define those?

Ms. LONGI. The municipalities.

Mr. WEBER. Municipalities.

Ms. LONGI. They are defined as municipalities. Right. And so the constitution enshrine that they will now have elected officials. And so those elections are slated for early 2017 or some time in 2017. So right now we are working with our State Department colleagues, our Embassy, other donors in the field to decide how we as the international community can help support and help the Tunisians make this transition decentralization a success. And so that is going to be a big push over the next year for our assistance as well as for the Tunisians as they work on this.

Another piece of that is to work with citizens, and civil society, and the private sector, on how to work with these new decentralized communities.

Mr. WEBER. Let's go back to what you are just now saying. You said you met with the stakeholders. You are talking about citizens, private sectors, NGOs? Can you name four or five different groups of stakeholders?

Ms. LONGI. Sure. NGOs, other civil society groups, private businesses that work in these areas, investors from abroad, investors from within Tunisia. So there is a lot of groups.

Mr. WEBER. Okay. And then one final question, if I may, Madam Chairman. I am going to run over just a second here. According to my notes, there was a lot of opposition, I guess as they were making a political transition. It says such as trade—from trade unions. What kind of trade unions? I mean, do they have—or is that electrical? Is that plumbing? Is that agricultural? Do you know?

Mr. DESROCHER. Yeah. Tunisia has a very potent trade union history, I guess I would say. The largest umbrella organization is something called the UGTT, and, in fact, the UGTT was one of the four members of the quartet that won the Nobel prize, the Nobel Peace prize, for their contribution to building the consensus that helped lead to this democratic revolution, this the post revolutionary period, the democratic governance.

The labor unions are—have considerable weight in Tunisia, and they are part of this dialogue about how to reform the economy.

Mr. WEBER. Name the kinds of labor. That is my——

Mr. DESROCHER. Sorry?

Mr. WEBER. Name the kinds of labor, that is my specific question——

Mr. DESROCHER. I think it would cover all those areas, teachers, government employees.

Mr. WEBER. Okay. So they have robust in place of unions?

Mr. DESROCHER. Yes. Yes, they do.

Mr. WEBER. Okay, great. That is it.

Thank you very much.

Ms. ROS-LEHTINEN. Thank you, Mr. Weber.

Ms. Frankel.

Ms. FRANKEL. Thank you, Madam Chair.

Thank you to the witnesses for being here.

Mr. Weber, I just want you to know, I did a Google search while you were asking your question. There is 16 non-NATO allies.

Mr. WEBER. Okay. I also did a Google search. Texas has 268,000 square miles, and Tunisia has 63,000 square. I am just saying.

Ms. FRANKEL. One other thing I would say to Mr. Deutch. You know what, when you told the results of the poll, I almost had to laugh only because I was thinking they would be the same results here in the United States of America, which is sort of ironic? Isn't it?

But I just came back from Tunisia. I was there with Mr. Royce. It was a very enlightening experience for me. And we, of course, met with a very able Ambassador Rubinstein. We met with the President of Tunisia, their Prime Minister, Interior Minister, their speaker of the Parliament and some of their members and they actually have—Madam Chairman had quite a few women parliamentarians.

We did go over to that museum, the Bardo, and we did a wreath ceremony. So just, you know, my impressions—I think my first—the good thing about going to other countries is actually, I find, not just going to meet with the President and the Prime Minister, but just the ride through whatever city you are in and just to see the people.

And you know what you see is just, you know, we saw hundreds and hundreds of people just trying to get about in their business, innocent people just trying to get about in their business.

And, you know what the impressions that were given to us, the people we spoke to was—which I will just underscore things you have emphasized, and some of my colleagues have is how—how two really bad terrorist attacks have almost devastated their tourism economy, the attack at the hotel, the attack at Bardo Museum. The hotel we stayed at which was quite lovely, there was nobody there. And this is the most beautiful coast in Tunisia.

We also got to meet with Ambassador Bodde, who was the virtual Ambassador from Libya. And we were able to have some good discussions on, really, the interrelationship between Tunisia and Libya and the fear of fighters coming back and forth and so forth.

And a couple of questions I had, because one of the points that were made, and I want to ask you about the weapons. I think Mr. Weber raised an issue there, was the—I thought the concern was about weapons that had fallen into wrong hands since the—in Libya rather than—is that an issue there?

Mr. DESROCHER. Well, I would say certainly, I mean, again, in Tunisia, control of weapons is not a tremendous concern of ours. Of course, like I say, we are continuously in touch with our Tunisian military counterparts as part of our security assistance program to talk about such things. But you are right, the weapons that were in the hands of the Qadhafi regime and their potential spread is something that we need to keep an eye on.

Ms. FRANKEL. And then the other question I had, which I think would be important really for this hearing and for the public. If you could just explain why we should care about Tunisia and what is going on in Tunisia and Libya. What is the importance of that region to the United States to our security, the security, and to the economy of our allies?

Mr. DESROCHER. And I invite you to chime in as well.

I think Tunisia is important to us for a number of reasons. The Tunisians have already built and are still building, you know, a very impressive democratic system in the face of great challenges and, you know, in the face of a history that is, you know, frankly, was not very supportive of democracy.

The Egyptians are trying to make that change. As we have seen through so much of the world making that transition to democracy is a very challenging thing. And I think it is in our interests to support that just as a general principle, and we do. And, of course, that aside, Tunisia is in a difficult region, most importantly, it has a very challenging neighbor in Libya and in the unstable situation in Libya, which, you know, the threat from that instability in Libya could potentially spread more broadly, which is certainly something we don't want to see. And it is very much in our interests to help our Tunisian friends prepare and strengthen not only their democracy, but their economy, and their security, in a way that helps them be a bull worker against that instability.

Ms. FRANKEL. Did you want to answer that?

Ms. LONGI. No.

Ms. FRANKEL. Okay. Thank you. Madam Chair, I yield back.

Ms. ROS-LEHTINEN. Thank you, Ms. Frankel.

Dr. Yoho.

Mr. YOHO. Thank you, Madam Chair. Good to seeing you. Thank you for being here. I find it interesting that there are fledging democracy that started with the Jasmine Revolution in 2011; the Arab Spring, the whole genesis of that. And then you see this fledging democracy building up, and things are going—what we would consider in the right way, and then we see the terrorist attacks that happened last summer and tourism is down 90 percent, the way I understand it and its kind of just floundering there and people aren't really flocking to get back there. And they have so much prime real estate, you know, from an American perspective looking at that. It is a beautiful part of the country.

If we look at that democracy and it is so important that we have a thriving democracy in there to show what liberty and freedoms can do. People that are striving to better their country like that. What have they done that is working, that we can learn from so that we can, you know, maybe have an influence or bolster that to effect, that they continue down that path? And what have they done that hasn't worked so that we don't make those mistakes when we are helping other countries that are fledging democracies that want to build from that?

And then a third question is, how much influence has the Muslim Brotherhood have in that country? And then I have got a couple more.

Mr. DESROCHER. I would point to a couple of factors. I mean, fundamentally, I think, what the Tunisians have done right is they have been guided by a sense of consensus and by a sense of, despite, perhaps, differing political or economic approaches, the sense of a need to move together and work together.

For example, I would highlight, you know, I mentioned before the Nobel Peace prize that was given to a quartet of organizations for the role they played in bringing together Tunisians to support the revolution. And this was a disparate group of people. It included both the trade union that I mentioned but it also the employers, an organization whose acronym is UTICA, which is the employers' union. And these are organizations that don't necessarily see eye to eye on, say, economic matters but definitely saw eye to eye along with their compatriots and the quartet, and Tunisia's political parties on the need to work together. And I think that we have seen that over the past few years as, you know, there is wide support—as difficult as these economic reforms are, there is wide support across the Tunisian political leadership for these reforms despite their difficulty.

And as basically to the role of political Islam, I would just note again, that we have talked a bit already about the role that

Ennahda is playing, and it is—as Mr. Deutch said, it made an announcement yesterday that it is splitting its civil and religious activities away from its political activities.

Mr. YOHO. Right.

Mr. DESROCHER. But it remains a political party with an Islamic bent, but it is one that has proven itself to work within the political system——

Mr. YOHO. Let me get Ms. Longi to weigh in on this. And if you focus on what have they done wrong that we can learn from that?

Ms. LONGI. What have they done wrong.

Mr. YOHO. Is it like a security issue, you know? Do they have border security? Do they have to crack down harder other terrorist or terrorist threats? You know, if you are looking at that country to continue the growth of a democracy, if you—to look at it, what would you say they shouldn't have done this and we should correct this—or they should correct it. I don't want to help them correct their——

Ms. LONGI. Well, USAID doesn't do the border security work.

Mr. YOHO. Okay.

Ms. LONGI. But I can say, and maybe this just gets to the right, but continues to be a challenge is the unemployment issue. Because the unemployment issue and combined with the security issues does create a real challenge for Tunisia to overcome a lot of this at once.

And so the pace of it probably may seem slow, but if you look how this, you know, new vibrant democracy is working, they have passed some very important private—or business reform laws that, over time, if they keep that commitment will help create those private sector jobs which will balance out.

Mr. YOHO. All right. Let me go back now to Mr. Desrocher. If you can tell us what they need to keep doing to bolster that democracy growing?

You know, I know we need to worry about the terrorist threats and security and things like that. I mean, what would you recommend?

Mr. DESROCHER. Well, I mean, I think Maria, you know, hit the point on the head. I think that the challenge that Tunisia faces is not so much that I can't point to, say, this mistake or that mistake, something that a decision should be different. What the real challenge is that the reforms, economic in governance building, in law enforcement, in security that need to move forward are things that—take time to implement.

And the economic situation there is challenging, the security situation there is challenging. And I know that Tunisians are moving as fast as they can, but it is really moving forward on those economic reforms to create jobs. Moving forward we are helping with reforms in the security sector so that they have civil police services that can enforce the law and enforce order while at the same time respecting civil rights and respecting the rule of law. Which is equally important.

And I guess if I were to sum up the challenge is that, you know, these kinds of reforms take time, and the difficult situation in Tunisia, means that time is very precious.

Mr. YOHO. Thank you.

Thank you, Madam Chair.

Ms. ROS-LEHTINEN. Thank you, Dr. Yoho.

Mr. Boyle.

Mr. BOYLE. Yes, thank you, Madam Chair and Ranking Member.

I wanted to ask you about two different issues, although you will I think pretty easily see the connection where I am going in a second.

The first is regarding the youth unemployment rate, which figures for 2015 show was estimated at 30 percent, remarkably high.

I was wondering to the extent that we know what is Tunisia doing right now to tackle this real problem?

Ms. LONGI. The passage of a lot of these foundational laws is one thing, because that is creating a better environment for the private sector to create jobs. Tunisia historically has had a very large public sector. And so the shift that they are making now is to encourage a stronger private sector where this job creation can actually take place, and so that is one thing.

Another thing that we have been working—the partnerships that we have included partnerships with the Minister of Employment and the Ministry of Education, because a lot of the reason for the youth unemployment is the mismatch between the jobs that are there and that can be created and the education that people are getting. And so we have worked to create some career centers, career development centers, within the universities, within the vocational schools to try to make that match better.

And so I think those are some of the challenges that exist and why the youth unemployment is so high. And we have seen great engagement and requests for assistance directly from ministers on this.

Mr. BOYLE. Well, the second question I am going to ask seem to be a natural flow is according to the U.N., and if you disagree with this, please let me know, but according to the U.N., there are currently 4,000 Tunisians fighting in Syria and about 1,500 fighting in Libya.

So I want to know what we believe the Tunisian Government is doing to champ down on this and extremism? And, of course, we see the connection between a country with a 30-percent youth unemployment rate and then also the problem of extremism in this region.

Ms. LONGI. I can start.

Mr. DESROCHER. Go ahead.

Ms. LONGI. We have been looking at the drivers of violent extremism in Tunisia. USAID, State Department, the Department of Defense, we are trying to figure out—and the reasons the drivers they are very local. Sometimes it is by neighborhood and sometimes by region. So the drivers that we've identified in certain areas of Tunisia include the unemployment, the disaffected population, including youth, some of the people not happy with the pace of reforms, people not happy with how their government is including them.

And so if you look at some of the programs, we are trying to target to address these, they include creating transparent and accountable local governments so people can—citizens can feel like they are a part of that. And so the employment is part of the solution as well as the citizen engagement. That is one way to address the specific drivers. There is a security aspect to it too.

Mr. DESROCHER. Yeah. I will just note, just add that I think that covers it very well but on the security aspect the Tunisians are taking measures to bolster the security along their border with Libya, which we are helping them with. There are ties to go back between Libya and Tunisia that go back quite some time in relationships and communications that go back quite some time and poses a special challenge, but the Tunisians are working hard, to in much of the way that that Maria discussed, in trying to find ways to identify those who might be tempted by these ideologies and detect people before they head for the airport, before they head across the border and to try to set up the systems that are in place at the borders to prevent these people from leaving.

But it is a serious challenge and it is going to take a long-term solution.

Mr. BOYLE. I will just say finally I get the impression, and correct me if I am wrong, but it seems as if you are both on the more optimistic realm of the spectrum if I were to characterize your comments. Would that be fair in terms of what the Tunisian Government is doing right now in the steps that they are taking?

Ms. LONGI. I am optimistic. The engagement that we have, if you just look and the economics here, the engagement from minister level to working level on really truly being committed to creating jobs, and improving the business environment and, to getting youth engaged in a constructive way, it is positive.

Mr. DESROCHER. I would definitely second that. I am optimistic because of the record that the Tunisians have built up over the past few years. They are pursuing the kinds of reforms that Maria described that they need to pursue. And these are not easy things to do but they are pursuing them despite the difficulty.

Mr. BOYLE. Thank you.

Ms. ROS-LEHTINEN. Thank you very much.

Does any member wish to have another round? Thank you so much.

Thank you for presenting a very realistic and hopeful outlook for our great partner Tunisia. Having been there also, I wish I would have been in Ms. Frankel's CODEL, but we went on our own and it was sad to see beautiful hotels empty.

We hope that folks come back to the beauty of Tunisia. Thank you so much.

And with that, the subcommittee is adjourned.

[Whereupon, at 3:37 p.m., the subcommittee was adjourned.]

APPENDIX

MATERIAL SUBMITTED FOR THE RECORD

SUBCOMMITTEE HEARING NOTICE
COMMITTEE ON FOREIGN AFFAIRS
U.S. HOUSE OF REPRESENTATIVES
WASHINGTON, DC 20515-6128

Subcommittee on the Middle East and North Africa
Ileana Ros-Lehtinen (R-FL), Chairman

May 18, 2016

TO: MEMBERS OF THE COMMITTEE ON FOREIGN AFFAIRS

You are respectfully requested to attend an OPEN hearing of the Committee on Foreign Affairs, to be held by the Subcommittee on the Middle East and North Africa in Room 2172 of the Rayburn House Office Building (and available live on the Committee website at http://www.ForeignAffairs.house.gov):

DATE: Wednesday, May 25, 2016

TIME: 2:30 p.m.

SUBJECT: Tunisia's Struggle for Stability, Security, and Democracy

WITNESSES: Mr. John Desrocher
Deputy Assistant Secretary for Egypt and Maghreb Affairs
Bureau of Near Eastern Affairs
U.S. Department of State

Ms. Maria Longi
Deputy Assistant Administrator
Bureau for the Middle East
U.S. Agency for International Development

By Direction of the Chairman

COMMITTEE ON FOREIGN AFFAIRS

MINUTES OF SUBCOMMITTEE ON _____ *the Middle East and North Africa* _____ HEARING

Day___ *Wednesday*___ Date____ *May 25, 2016*___ Room_____ *2172*_____

Starting Time ___ *2:37 p.m.*___ Ending Time ___ *3:37 p.m.*___

Recesses [_____] (____to ____) (____to ____) (____to ____) (____to ____) (____to ____) (____to ____)

Presiding Member(s)

Chairman Ros-Lehtinen

Check all of the following that apply:

Open Session ☑
Executive (closed) Session ☐
Televised ☑

Electronically Recorded (taped) ☑
Stenographic Record ☑

TITLE OF HEARING:

Tunisia's Struggle for Stability, Security, and Democracy

SUBCOMMITTEE MEMBERS PRESENT:

Chairman Ros-Lehtinen, Reps. Weber and Yoho
Ranking Member Deutch, Reps. Frankel and Boyle

NON-SUBCOMMITTEE MEMBERS PRESENT: *(Mark with an * if they are not members of full committee.)*

HEARING WITNESSES: Same as meeting notice attached? Yes ☑ No ☐
(If "no", please list below and include title, agency, department, or organization.)

STATEMENTS FOR THE RECORD: *(List any statements submitted for the record.)*

TIME SCHEDULED TO RECONVENE _____
or
TIME ADJOURNED ___ *3:37 p.m.*___

Subcommittee Staff Director